God Bless

JL

I dedicate this book to my family. I want to thank my wife for being by my side on this journey together. Charmaine, you have been a model of consistent love through all of my ups and downs. I want to thank my children Jomo, Jamya and Josiah for providing me with so much good material and teaching me unconditional love. I want to honor my parents for without them I would not be here. Both of my parents are gone now, but I will never forget the impact they made on my life. And I am thankful for the church God has called me to, Love First Christian Center. I love you all.

God bless

Dr. Jomo Cousins

Introduction

You may be asking yourself "What does Jomo Cousins know about success"? The answer is quite simple, I am a walking, talking, breathing example of success. Not because of money or fame, but because of perseverance.

I graduated High School with a C average; yet I now have a PhD in Religious Theology. I never played football in high school; yet I was drafted into the National Football League. As a young man, faith was the furthest thing in my mind; but by God's grace we have built a debt free ministry. Two years ago I was a Stage 3 Cancer Patient; I stand before you today as a Stage 3 Cancer Survivor. Success is not only the action of succeeding, but it is how you recover and respond to failures and setbacks.

I believe (1) there are certain tools that when used correctly will lead you to success, (2) I know that God wants you to be successful, and finally (3) I want to show you that success leaves clues. Many people are looking for success in the form of a magic pill or potion.

I'm not claiming to be "the know it all" for everything, rather I am a man looking to help define the "**A, B, C's of Success**". To accomplish this, my first thought was to *define* words associated with success. For without definition we have no purpose. I believe the definition of the word based on English terminology is important, but we must also look at how the *Bible* defines success in relation to the word. For the Bible is inspired by God and is a book of wisdom from on high. I have also included several *relevant stories* that I believe will demonstrate the importance of the word in the journey towards success. As always, I will give you *real life applications* of the word; break it down and put it all back together. Each chapter will contain famous *quotes* that will reinforce the thoughts presented and help you to see how the Word will lead you to success.

With that being said, let the journey towards success begin.

A

Ability
1: the quality or state of being able
2: competence in doing, skill
3: natural aptitude or acquired proficiency

1 Peter 4:10 (AMP)

10 As each of you has received a gift (a particular spiritual talent, a gracious divine endowment), employ it for one another as [befits] good trustees of God's many-sided grace [faithful stewards of the extremely diverse powers and gifts granted to Christians by unmerited favor].

The scripture lets us know that the gift is already ours. In this sense, our gift is our *ability* to do things with excellence and ease. Because our *ability* comes so naturally, often times we belittle the impact.
It is common to us; therefore, we are unable to recognize the true greatness in our gift.

Throughout my adult life it always seemed that I would end up in front of an audience.

People acknowledged my *ability* to communicate. But I would say, "I am just running my mouth," which I was, because I did not understand this was my gift.

What was easy to me was not easy to most. This was a key realization. I had to get to a point where I was able to acknowledge my *ability;* and in my *ability*, I would be able to define my future.

Listen family, your *ability* will define your future.

In today's society we have so much technology available in the palm of our hands. Whether you have an Apple or an Android, you most likely have the capability to use apps on your phone. In most cases, the phones are pre-loaded with some of the most popular apps.

During one visit to my father's house, my step-brother John came by while I was there. John and I were the closest in age of all the brothers and sisters in this "Brady Bunch". John had finally fulfilled his childhood dream and become a pilot.

During this particular visit, John pulled out his iPad and was showing me all of the airports and landing patterns that he had traveled. I was amazed as I looked at his iPad; it was full of apps. He had at least four screens of applications. He had a 16 GB iPad that was full of information and I had a 64 GB that was barely used. His iPad was so full that he even had an app for extra storage. Looking at his iPad I felt incomplete, for I have never gotten off the first page with mine. I basically use my iPad as a teaching tool. After seeing my brother's iPad (which has less storage), be utilized far more, I started to question whether it was my iPad's fault for lack of utilization or mine? I came to an obvious conclusion. My iPad had tremendous <u>ability</u> that I could access, if I just utilized the apps. The apps have the potential to increase my <u>ability</u> as a teacher, just as John has used them to increase his <u>ability</u> as a pilot.

There is an ancient proverb "familiarity breeds contempt".

When things become common we no longer pay them the proper respect.

I believe Jesus said it best in **Luke 4:24 (NLT); "But I tell you the truth, no prophet is accepted in his own hometown."**

We all need someone in our circle that will recognize our _ability_ when we are unable to see the gift that God has given. Your _ability_ is your God given gift; once it is identified, you will find your wealthy place. Common things will lead to a common life. Don't despise your _ability_; embrace it. For in your _ability_, you will determine what sets you apart from others; what makes you unique; your purpose.

"There are two great days in a person's life- the day we are born and the day we discover why." William Barclay

We all have God-given abilities. The challenge of life is identifying the _ability_ that can be used for its greatest good for the betterment of society.

"If you focus on making a difference, the dollars will follow. If you focus on making a dollar, you won't make a difference and you won't make many dollars." Tye Maner

We have all been in a situation where we needed to make a call but our cell phone battery had run out of power. This is a classic example of having the _ability_, but not having the power. God has endowed us with the _ability_ and the power to perform.

Philippians 2:13 (AMP)

13 [Not in your own strength] for it is God Who is all the while effectually at work in you [energizing and creating in you the power and desire], both to will and to work for His good pleasure and satisfaction and delight.

We were created on purpose by God to serve a purpose. We must live in our _ability_ and place no limits on our potential. If we don't put a limit on God, God won't put a limit on us. We are the biggest obstacle in our journey to success.

Philippians 4:13 (NLT)

13 For I can do everything through Christ, [a] who gives me strength

I repeat, if you don't put a limit on God, God will not put a limit on you.

Many people never use the applications on their devices to their maximum potential. The device has the *ability* to provide resources at the tips of our fingers. But, it is our decision to utilize the device to its greatest capability. I want you to know that God has given you millions of apps. You were born with them, and it's up to you to use them.

B

Belief

1: a state or habit of mind in which trust or confidence is placed in some person or thing **2:** conviction of the truth of some statement or the reality of some being or phenomenon especially when based on examination of evidence

John 20: 24-28 (AMP)

24 But Thomas, one of the Twelve, called the Twin, was not with them when Jesus came. 25 So the other disciples kept telling him, We have seen the Lord! But he said to them, Unless I see in His hands the marks made by the nails and put my finger into the nail prints, and put my hand into His side, I will never believe [it]. 26 Eight days later His disciples were again in the house, and Thomas was with them. Jesus came, though they were behind closed doors, and stood among them and said, Peace to you!

27 Then He said to Thomas, Reach out your finger here, and see My hands; and put out your hand and place [it] in My side.

***Do not be faithless and incredulous, but
[stop your unbelief and] believe! 28 Thomas
answered Him, My Lord and my God!***

Isn't it amazing that even though Thomas
walked with Jesus and witnessed Jesus
perform many miracles he chose not to
believe? We must be very careful when it
comes to *belief*. God will meet you on your
level of *belief* and you will live on the level in
which you believe.

Question: How are you living? For the way
that you are living is in direct proportion to
your believing.

Each of us has a *belief* system that has been
established as a result of life experiences. It is
critical that we evaluate our *belief* system to
confirm that it matches the path we have
envisioned in our mind. If the desired path is
not positive, bold, and courageous; it is likely
that the level of your *belief* is low.

Remember, God will meet you at the level of
your *belief*, therefore if you have minimal
belief the likelihood of finding success on that
path drops substantially.

There is an old African story that says, "If you take a baby elephant, place a chain around one of its back legs, hook the chain to a stake, and drive that stake into the ground to restrain the baby elephant until it's big enough to fend for itself, then when the caretaker removes both the stake and the chain from the elephant's back leg, the elephant will not venture out beyond the length of the chain that once restrained him. The story goes on to say that the elephant has been conditioned to accept residency in a mental prison given to him by his caretaker."

They say elephants have great memories and never forget anything. This chained elephant allowed his past chains to paralyze his future dreams.

I wonder how many of us have allowed past failure to limit future dreams.

"Whether you think you can, or you think you can't-- you're right." Henry Ford

Matthew 8:13 (AMP)

**13 Then to the centurion Jesus said, Go; it
shall be done for you as you have believed.
And the servant boy was restored to health at
that very [a]moment.**

Jesus again makes it plain that our _belief_
system will manifest based on the things that
we desire and ask for with pure motives. We
will move in the direction of our most
dominate thought. So, make sure you are
focusing your thoughts in the right direction.
We can interpret the verse; "it shall be done
for you as you have believed" to mean; we
must believe it is so, when it is not so; in
order for it to be so.

I repeat; we must believe it is so, when it is
not so, in order for it to be so.

*Long ago, there was a battle about to take
place. One of the generals was talking about
tactics with his team of officers. An officer
interrupted him and explained that he thought
that the strategy was a waste of time. "The
gods have already decided who will win." he
proclaimed.*

"Are you suggesting that fate has decided the result in advance?" the general asked. "Yes, I am." the officer responded. The general took a coin out of his pocket and said, "So if I toss this coin and it comes up heads, we win, but if it's tails we lose.

Is that how fate works?" "Pretty much." said the officer. The general tossed the coin and it came up heads. "See, the gods have decided. We can't lose now!" They went to their troops with the good news and the soldiers marched into battle with renewed enthusiasm. After a glorious victory, the officers met in the general's tent to celebrate. "Do you believe in fate now?" the general was asked. The leader smiled, reached into his pocket and pulled out the coin to show to the others. It was heads on both sides. "No, I don't believe in fate, just the value of self-belief. When the soldiers thought that we couldn't lose, I knew that we couldn't lose."

I share this adapted story with you today to encourage you to believe in yourself, to have confidence in your abilities and to launch yourself into the fray with energy and enthusiasm.

If you do, great victories will be won.

"The greatest danger for most of us is not that our aim is too high and we miss it, but that it is too low and we reach it." *Michelangelo*

Family, let's aim high. Let your belief in God's abilities help you to soar to heights you could never achieve on your own.

C

Courage
1: the ability to do something that you know is difficult or dangerous

Joshua 1:6-9 (AMP)

6 Be strong (confident) and of good courage, for you shall cause this people to inherit the land which I swore to their fathers to give them. 7 Only you be strong and very courageous, that you may do according to all the law which Moses My servant commanded you. Turn not from it to the right hand or to the left that you may prosper wherever you go. 8 This Book of the Law shall not depart out of your mouth, but you shall meditate on it day and night, that you may observe and do according to all that is written in it. For then you shall make your way prosperous, and then you shall deal wisely and have good [b]success. 9 Have not I commanded you? Be strong, vigorous, and very courageous. Be not afraid, neither be dismayed, for the Lord your God is with you wherever you go.

This is one of my favorite passages in the Bible for it deals with life transitions.

At some point in time, we all experience transitions. I have found that many times the transition does not occur at a convenient time. For example, there is never a good time to lose a job, home, spouse, child or a myriad of other possibilities. But those things happen and you must pick up the pieces of your life. In this scripture, we see God telling Joshua it is your time, be of good _courage_. Most of the successful people you see are courageous. They were willing to take the chances most people would never take which is why they are successful.

Question: What's holding you back? Is it a lack of _courage_?

Listen family, there are only two options, you fly or you fall, but staying in the nest is guaranteed failure.

Courage does not mean being fearless.

Courage means stepping out on faith and believing the unseen.

"In 1994, during the presidential-election campaign, Mandela got on a tiny propeller plane to fly down to the killing fields of Natal and give a speech to his Zulu supporters. I agreed to meet him at the airport, where we would continue our work after his speech. When the plane was 20 minutes from landing, one of its engines failed. Some on the plane began to panic. The only thing that calmed them was looking at Mandela, who quietly read his newspaper as if he were a commuter on his morning train to the office. The airport prepared for an emergency landing, and the pilot managed to land the plane safely. When Mandela and I got in the backseat of his bulletproof BMW that would take us to the rally, he turned to me and said, "Man, I was terrified up there!"

Mandela was terrified but he didn't show it. _Courage_ is the act of understanding the magnitude of the challenge but not allowing your emotions to dictate your decisions. In the verse, Joshua was told by God to rise up for it was his time. His leader Moses had passed on and all that Joshua learned and endured was to prepare him for this time.

You will notice that God kept repeating "Be strong and of good courage"; I believe God is speaking that same message to us today.

God told Joshua to meditate and to stay focused. Meditating on the Word of God is so critical; for it allows the Word to take root in your heart. So when challenges arise, and they will, you will have the boldness to speak _courage_ to your situation. When we are unfamiliar with the Word of God it creates a lack of understanding; we are unable to accurately understand and realize God's plan for our lives. Therefore we are unable to truly stand on _courage_; which is the reason many of us fail to accomplish our goals.

"Courage is the most important of all the virtues because without courage, you can't practice any other virtue consistently."
Maya Angelou

D

Discipline
1: orderly or prescribed conduct or pattern of behavior, self-control

Hebrews 12:11 (AMP)

11 For the time being no discipline brings joy, but seems grievous and painful; but afterwards it yields a peaceable fruit of righteousness to those who have been trained by it [a harvest of fruit which consists in righteousness—in conformity to God's will in purpose, thought, and action, resulting in right living and right standing with God].

I want to identify two critical words in the definition: order and self-control.

Both are essential to the life of a successful person. Order is the system or pattern by which you accomplish a set task. Your order doesn't have to make sense to everyone, as long as it makes sense to you and provides the proper results.

Self-control is the mastery of self, in reference to limiting your limitations.

We all have limitations in various areas of our lives, but successful people are able to identify the limitations and make them strengths.

As you read this passage you will see there is usually little to no joy when you are becoming disciplined. The true benefits come later on down the line.

"There are two types of pain you will go through in life, the pain of discipline and the pain of regret. Discipline weighs ounces while regret weighs tons." Jim Rohn

We all struggle with *discipline* in some manner; whether it's dietary, punctuality or just life in general. *Discipline* doesn't come natural, but as a result of learning through painful consequences. Whether it is the flight you missed or the doctor's orders you don't want to receive, *discipline* keeps showing up. *Discipline* is choosing to say yes, when your mind, body and soul are saying no.

Lebron James has been called the "greatest NBA player of all time". A player known for his dominating play; which many attributed to his size.

During the off season, Lebron changed his diet "I had no sugars, no dairy, I had no carbs. All I ate was meat, fish, veggies and fruit. That's it. For 67 straight days". Lebron's social media accounts showcased his new eating habits, including his determination "Thank you #Nammos My Konos for the dessert gesture. Too dang on bad I can't eat it! Grrrrrrrrrr! Smh. #ButIWantItThough #AlmostAtTheFinishLine"

Lebron's new diet is a clear example of *discipline*; a display of self-control despite the temptations that are thrown your way. Many may dismiss his success by saying, "he has money", or "he has a private chef". Although true, at the end of the day Lebron had to decide that he will stay focused on his chosen path. Lebron had to learn a new way of eating, which required *discipline*.

Question: Are you being disciplined and living towards God's plan?

Proverbs 12:1 (NLT)

1 To learn, you must love discipline; it is stupid to hate correction.

"Success is tons of discipline." Al Tomsik

"Do what you should do, when you should do it, whether you feel like it or not"
Thomas Huxley

"Self-discipline is the key to personal greatness. It is the magic quality that opens all doors for you, and makes everything else possible. With self-discipline, the average person can rise as far and as fast as his talents and intelligence can take him. But without self-discipline, a person with every blessing of background, education and opportunity will seldom rise above mediocrity." Brian Tracy

"No stream or gas drives anything until it is confined. No Niagara is ever turned into light and power until it is tunneled. No life ever grows great until it is focused, dedicated and disciplined." Harry E. Fosdick

Family, I challenge you to identify some areas in your life that are undisciplined. Here are some steps that I have used to help me be more disciplined:

1. Identify areas of undisciplined behavior
2. Seek wisdom from those who have mastered that area, i.e. books or mentors
3. Seek someone you respect to hold you accountable
4. Give yourself grace to grow; you will fall short at times

Remember this: what we don't confront will not change and what we do not change, we allow. We must never complain about what we allow.

Change begins with you.

E

Endurance

1: the ability to do something difficult for a long time

2: the ability to deal with pain or suffering that continues for a long time

James 1:4 (AMP)

4 But let endurance and steadfastness and patience have full play and do a thorough work, so that you may be [people] perfectly and fully developed [with no defects], lacking in nothing.

<u>Endurance</u> is something not often sought by individuals throughout their lifetime. Most of us are chasing after money, love and power. But no one I know says to them self, "I wish I had more *endurance*". Opportunities to build <u>endurance</u> are usually not planned and initially they are not desired, but when properly understood they are tremendously beneficial.

Oftentimes, <u>endurance</u> is strengthened by failures, disappointments and seemingly unpleasant moments in life.

It takes a strong person to overcome the hurt, understand the lesson learned and exercise the will to keep going to build *endurance*.

The power of *endurance* is never really recognized or acknowledged until the benefits start to manifest, but people often never get to reap the reward before they quit. When I first started ministry, I thought there were already enough churches. I asked God what was going to make our ministry different; I wanted our focus to be something that would last. The Spirit of the Lord led me to scripture.

Matthew 21:13 (AMP)

13 My house shall be called a house of prayer.

I decided that we were going to build our house on the power of prayer. Then, I asked God in what manner did He want me to deliver His message. I was led to a teleconference line that I was already using for business purposes.
God, in His infinite wisdom had everything that I needed already within my grasp.

*Then I told God that I was going to do prayer
every Monday morning like I used to do with
the business; I called it "Monday morning
motivation". But I couldn't get peace, I felt
as if God wanted me to do it more than one
day a week. I prayed on it and felt like God
was telling me to do it Monday through
Friday. I knew what God was telling me, but
I didn't want to commit. I didn't want to
endure waking up early five days a week. I
finally relented, knowing that I couldn't
outbox God and started the prayer line
Monday through Friday as He instructed.*

*It has been eight years since I started the
prayer line. In those eight years, I have been
late, overslept, missed a day or two along the
way; but I have not stopped. People listen to
me praying from around the world five days a
week. Why? Because I had the endurance to
get past the bad days, the tired days, the sick
days, the trials that life brings and kept
praying. My endurance is now bearing fruit.*

1 Thessalonians 5:17 (AMP)

17 be unceasing and persistent in prayer.

Endurance is going to take you past your limits and it will often reveal strength you never knew that you had. Anything worth having is worth enduring. My wife has blessed our home with three wonderful children, but for us to have these gifts she had to endure nine months of pregnancy. We should not expect success without *endurance*.

The key to all success is having the *endurance* to fight through all obstacles and realize the game is not over until you win. Thomas Edison failed more than 10,000 times before he created the light bulb. Because of his *endurance*, he was able to create 1093 patents; the phonograph, the motion picture camera, typewriting machines, telephones and many more.

"Our greatest weakness lies in giving up. The most certain way to succeed is always to try just one more time." Thomas Edison

Thomas Edison was not detoured by failure; in fact he was motivated by failure. Failure provided him with the *endurance* to keep trying, keep pushing and to stay after his goal of success.

Anything worth having in this life will take _endurance_ to achieve. We should not expect success without _endurance_.

F

Failure

1: lack of success
2: a falling short: deficiency <a crop
failure>

Proverbs 24:16 (NLT)

*16 The godly may trip seven times, but they
will get up again. But one disaster is enough
to overthrow the wicked.*

In this verse we see that you are exempt from
eternal failing, just because you are Godly.
We will all fail in different areas of our life;
that is a fact of life. The true question is; will
we allow that *failure* to be a definer or a
refiner? I have seen so many people allow a
particular *failure* to define their whole life;
not realizing that the failure was supposed to
be a comma in their life and not a period. We
must not allow what was supposed to be a
drive through to turn into a buffet.

There are some seasons in life that we just
have to keep on moving through and not park
there.

Listen family, *failure* does not discriminate; it will eventually show up at your door.

The verse mentions seven times, seven being the number of completion. This verse is saying that when you make a complete fall, complete miss up or complete *failure* it doesn't have to stop what God has in store for you.

Failure is not final; *failure* is a part of the process towards success. Everything worth having is hard and on occasion it is accompanied by *failure* as you learn the process. Whether we are talking or walking, riding a bike, or driving, everything starts out hard and requires effort before it becomes easy.

Tyler Perry is an actor, producer, director, screenwriter, playwright, author and songwriter. He is also no stranger to failure.

Tyler Perry recently wrote to that effect in an email letter he sent to his fan base. "Do you know how many times I tried to be successful at doing plays before it finally worked? From 1992 until 1998, every show I put on flopped. No one showed up, and I lost all my money.

I wanted to give up. I thought I had failed, but the truth is, I never failed. Each and every time the show didn't work, I learned something new. I learned what not to do and what I could do better," wrote Perry, whose first staged play, "I Know I've Been Changed" was considered a financial failure when it first debuted in 1992 before he revamped it and found success taking it on the road and touring from 1998 to 2000.

The Gospel playwright made his foray into films transposing many of his straight-to-DVD stage productions into screen gems, dating back to 2001 when he introduced his play "Diary of a Mad Black Woman" to wide audiences via DVDs that were sold on his Web site. It was the $50.7 million box office success of his 2005 debut "Diary of a Mad Black Woman" that landed him a lucrative first-look, multiyear distribution deal with Lionsgate Entertainment.

The rest is history as they say, with the Hollywood writer/director/producer powerhouse churning out 17 films in 10 years, which have a lifetime gross of about $845 million worldwide, and six television shows.

"You have to understand that what you may perceive to be a failure may very well be an

opportunity to learn, grow, get better, and prepare for the next level. If you find the lessons in what you perceive to be failures, then you won't ever fail at anything," said Perry. "Everything I learned during the "learning" years (that's what I call them now) has helped me in the "harvest" years (that's what I'm living in now). Don't be hard on yourself. You haven't failed. Find the lesson so you can use it when you get to your harvest."

I share this story, to say that if you accelerate the number of attempts you make, you can accelerate your path to success.

Philippians 1:6 (AMP)

6 And I am convinced and sure of this very thing, that He Who began a good work in you will continue until the day of Jesus Christ [right up to the time of His return], developing [that good work] and perfecting and bringing it to full completion in you.

I love how the verse makes it clear, we are all under construction and none of us are complete.

Total completion comes when we meet Jesus, so stop focusing on others and start focusing on you.

Simon Cowell had a failed record company. By his late twenties, Cowell had made a million dollars and lost a million dollars. Cowell told The Daily Mail in 2012, "'I've had many failures. The biggest were at times when I believed my own hype. I'd had smaller failures, signing bands that didn't work, but my record company going bust that was the first big one."

Even after such a momentous loss, Cowell picked himself up and became one of the biggest forces in reality television, serving as a judge for "Pop Idol," "The X Factor," "Britain's Got Talent" and "American Idol."

Forbes has estimated his net worth at $95 million.

"Success is not final, failure is not fatal: it is the courage to continue that counts."
Winston Churchill

G

Goal
1: the terminal point of a race
2: the end toward which effort is
directed: aim

Philippians 3:13-14 (AMP)

*13 I do not consider, brethren, that I have
captured and made it my own [yet]; but one
thing I do [it is my one aspiration]:
forgetting what lies behind and straining
forward to what lies ahead, 14 I press on
toward the goal to win the [supreme and
heavenly] prize to which God in Christ Jesus
is calling us upward.*

If you lack aim, then you will never
successfully score a *goal*. *Goals* are a vital
part of achievement; they provide a clear view
and focus. I see goals as steps on the ladders
of life moving us up to the next level in life.

My first *goal* was to graduate from high
school, then college and so on and so forth.

Every _goal_ that you achieve should elevate you in life.

I recently read a story of a young lady who is blindly racing towards her _goal_.

"I love to cut pictures out of the local newspaper. One Saturday I found a very special picture in the paper, depicting a high school freshman as she prepares for a track meet.

With shoulder length brown hair, she looks like most runners her own age, thin, focused, intent on the race ahead. Undistracted, her face turned downward, she holds one hand at her right ear. In the other, she carries a tiny radio attached to a fanny pack. Nearby her father, Matt McCarthy, speaks into a small transmitter.

Natalie McCarthy, the ordinary looking girl in the picture, sprints both the one hundred and two hundred meter dashes for her Steilacoom High School track team; but that is not what makes her extraordinary. It is her almost total blindness that makes her most extraordinary.

So, how does she do it? How does she line up with a group of healthy, sighted teens and dash for a finish line she cannot see?

By radio.
Natalie runs with a single earpiece in her
right ear. With her father's voice coming
through the tiny transmitter, she hears the
course corrections he gives her from the
sidelines. With nothing more than trust, and
her father's verbal directions, Natalie runs at
full speed toward a goal she cannot see, with
competitors she can only hear, over obstacles
she can only imagine."

Here is a perfect picture of our race with God. For us, the Holy Spirit directs our race. We face challenges we cannot see. We race towards a _goal_ that we can only imagine. Though we don't hear our coach through a radio earpiece, the Lord promises over and over that He will guide us in our race for the finish line. He will direct us. We will hear our Heavenly Father's voice. We must trust and respond to the changing course, run the race; for your Father is whispering in your ear.

We must continuously set new _goals_; each one more challenging then the last. Our daily purpose is to achieve the _goals_ we have set before ourselves based on the words that God is whispering in our ears.

This means that we must be prepared to listen to the word that God is speaking. Every now and then we get too busy living and we need an extra push to set and achieve our *goals*.

Anthony Burgess was forty when he learned that he had only one year to live. He had a brain tumor that would kill him within a year. He knew he had a battle on his hands. He was completely financially broke at the time and he didn't have anything to leave his wife, Lynne, soon to be a widow.

Burgess had never been a professional novelist in the past, but he always knew that potential was inside him to be a writer. So, for the sole purpose of leaving royalties behind for his wife, he put a piece of paper into a typewriter and began writing. He had no certainty that he would even be published, but he couldn't think of anything else to do.

"It was January of 1960," he said "and according to the prognosis, I had a winter and spring and summer to live through, and would die with the fall of the leaf."

In that time, Burgess wrote energetically, finishing five and a half novels before the year was through (very nearly the entire lifetime output of E.M. Forster, and almost twice that of J.D. Salinger.)

But Burgess did not die. His cancer had gone into remission and then disappeared altogether. In his long and full life as a novelist (he is best known for "A Clock-work Orange") he wrote more than 70 books, but without the death sentence from cancer, he may not have written at all.

Many of us are like Anthony Burgess, hiding greatness inside, waiting for some external emergency to bring it out. Ask yourself, what would you do if you received Anthony Burgess' initial prognosis?

Question: If you have just one year to live, how would you live differently? What exactly would you do?

The concept of setting *goals* may be easy; the action of achieving that *goal* is the difficult part.

There are five key points that are important when setting a *goal*; be specific, the goal should be measurable, attainable, and relevant and time bound.

"A goal without a plan is just a wish."
Antoine de Saint-Exupery

"A dream without a goal is a wish with no plan and doomed to failure." Anonymous

"Nothing can stop the man with the right mental attitude from achieving his goal; nothing on Earth can help the man with the wrong mental attitude." Thomas Jefferson

H

Help

1: to give assistance or support to

Isaiah 41:10 (AMP)

10 Fear not [there is nothing to fear], for I am with you; do not look around you in terror and be dismayed, for I am your God. I will strengthen and harden you to difficulties, yes, I will help you; yes, I will hold you up and retain you with My [victorious] right hand of rightness and justice.

"I need *help*" is a statement that most people hesitate to use; mainly out of fear for appearing weak or unqualified. I believe that it takes strength to ask for *help*, because you are allowing yourself to be vulnerable. He who does not ask for *help* cannot grow. Understanding that you will never accomplish your goals in life without the *help* of others is a huge part of growing.

We all need role models and mentors to guide us through this maze that we call life.

Many fools try to do it on their own, but wise people seek counsel. Why live it, when you can read it. Getting <u>help</u> accelerates your growth.

Proverbs 11:14 (MSG)

14 Without good direction, people lose their way; the more wise counsel you follow, the better your chances.

This passage reminds us that we must seek wise counsel and not try to live life on our own. There are times when we try to live on our own and we unnecessarily drown.

So there's this huge flood one day and an entire town looks like it's going to be swallowed up by the waters. The police and other rescue agencies are running all over the place trying to get people to safety. So they send the rescue boat over to this house where a guy is sitting on the roof with the water lapping around his ankles and they say "Come on, quickly, there isn't much time." To which he says "Nah, its ok, God will provide."

So about an hour later they're zooming past in the boat again and they notice the guy is still there, only the water is up to his waist and almost to the top of the roof. "Quick", they say, "Get in the boat; it's going to get worse before it gets better." Once again, he replies "Nah, its ok, God will provide." An hour after that a rescue helicopter flies over the area and notices the guy, who must be standing on the peak of the roof now with only his head and shoulders above water. "Grab the rope", they cry, "It's your only hope!" The guy replies calmly "Don't worry, God will provide."

So the guy drowns and he goes to Heaven. He is a little ticked off with God for drowning him like that and expresses his concern, "I had faith, I believed in you and still you didn't help me!" God replies "Help you? What more did you want? I sent two boats and a helicopter!"

Family, yes God will always provide and oftentimes that looks like receiving *help* when you need it most.

It requires you to be open to receive that *help*.

It also means that we must believe when God tells us He is here to _help_!

So this guy's rollerblading down a mountain (not smart, but who am I to judge) when he sails off the edge of the cliff into the air. Just before he plummets to the ground, he manages to catch hold of the root of a tree which is hanging out of the cliff. So he's hanging there and isn't really sure what he's going to do. His arms are getting tired; he can't hold on for much longer. There's no way to climb up and no ledge to stand on.

When he hears a voice calling to him "Dave"; a bit surprised he says "Yes, is someone up there?" The voice replies "yes, there is". Relieved, Dave replies "Help me! I can't hold on much longer". The voice replies "I know you can't. That's why I'm here to save you." Dave says "Do I know you" and the voice says "Of course you do. It's me, God." Dave says "God?" To which he replies "Yes and I've come to save you. You do believe in me, don't you?" Dave replies "Oh yes God! Now, please throw down a rope." God immediately replies "But I'm God. I don't need a rope to save you Dave. You believe in me, don't you?"

Dave replies "Of course I do". God says "Good. Now all I want you to do is let go of the root and I'll catch you and bring you back to the top of the cliff." Hesitantly, Dave says "Uhhh" to which God replies "You do believe in me, don't you".

So Dave thinks about this for a few seconds and yells "is there anyone else up there"?

Of course this is a funny joke but it is also very truthful. Think about how many times God offered you _help_. But the _help_ didn't come as you expected, so you rejected it.

Question: How many of us are holding on to something despite God telling us to let go?

Family, we must receive the _help_ that God is offering.

We must walk by faith which means accepting _help_ when we may not understand how it will help us to reach our outcome. We may not know but God does.

"A man's pride can be his downfall, and he needs to learn when to turn to others for support and guidance." Bear Grylls

I

Inspiration

1: a divine influence or action on a person believed to qualify him or her to receive and communicate sacred revelation

2: the action or power of moving the intellect or emotions

3: the act of influencing or suggesting opinions

2 Timothy 3:16 (AMP)

16 Every Scripture is God-breathed (given by His inspiration) and profitable for instruction, for reproof and conviction of sin, for correction of error and discipline in obedience, [and] for training in righteousness (in holy living, in conformity to God's will in thought, purpose, and action)

I believe this verse encapsulates the message of God; which is why it is one of my favorites. Every, meaning nothing left out, is inspired by God.

So God's message is a message of *inspiration*.

Now, you may not like the message but the message was meant to inspire you to be the best you that you can be. Outside of God, you will never be all that He has called you to be.

Family, I want you to think about the thing that makes you come alive
Why do you do what you do every day?
When you wake in the morning; what is your desire to fulfill?

The answers to these questions are an indication of your <u>inspiration</u>; your driving force behind the qualities, desires and rationale that make you who you are.

Many think of *inspiration* as something monumental; something earth shaking. *Inspiration* can come in the form of a quick word, moment of truth or unexpected actions. I once read a story that inspired the author to go to breakfast.

A Thousand Marbles

The older I get, the more I enjoy Saturday mornings. Perhaps it's the quiet solitude that comes with being the first to rise, or maybe it's the unbounded joy of not having to be at work. Either way, the first few hours of a Saturday morning are most enjoyable. A few weeks ago, I was shuffling toward the kitchen with a steaming cup of coffee in one hand and the morning paper in the other. What began as a typical Saturday morning turned into one of those lessons that life seems to hand you from time to time.

Let me tell you about it. I turned the volume up on my radio in order to listen to a Saturday morning talk show. I heard an older sounding chap with a golden voice. You know the kind, he sounded like he should be in the broadcasting business himself. He was talking about "a thousand marbles" to someone named "Tom". I was intrigued and sat down to listen to what he had to say.

"Well, Tom, it sure sounds like you're busy with your job. I'm sure they pay you well but it's a shame you have to be away from home and your family so much. Hard to believe a young fellow should have to work sixty or seventy hours a week to make ends meet. Too bad you missed your daughter's dance recital." He continued,

"Let me tell you something Tom, something that has helped me keep a good perspective on my own priorities." And that's when he began to explain his theory of a "thousand marbles."

"You see, I sat down one day and did a little arithmetic. The average person lives about seventy-five years. With some living more and some live less, but on average, folks live about seventy-five years."

"Now then, I multiplied 75 times 52 and I came up with 3900 which is the number of Saturdays that the average person has in their entire lifetime. Now stick with me Tom, I'm getting to the important part." "It took me until I was fifty-five years old to think about all this in any detail", he went on, "and by that time I had lived through over twenty-eight hundred Saturdays. I got to thinking that if I lived to be seventy-five, I only had about a thousand of them left to enjoy." "So I went to a toy store and bought every single marble they had. I ended up having to visit three toy stores to round-up 1000 marbles. I took them home and put them inside of a large, clear plastic container right here in my workshop next to the radio.

Every Saturday since then, I have taken one marble out and throw it away." "I found that by watching the marbles diminish, I focused more on the really important things in life. There is nothing like watching your time here on this earth run out to help get your priorities straight."

"Now let me tell you one last thing before I sign-off with you and take my lovely wife out for breakfast. This morning, I took the very last marble out of the container. I figure if I make it until next Saturday then I have been given a little extra time. And the one thing we can all use is a little more time."

"It was nice to talk to you Tom, I hope you spend more time with your loved ones, and I hope to meet you again someday. Have a good morning!" You could have heard a pin drop when he finished. Even the show's moderator didn't have anything to say for a few moments. I guess he gave us all a lot to think about. I had planned to do some work that morning, and then go to the gym. Instead, I went upstairs and woke my wife up with a kiss.

"C'mon honey, I'm taking you and the kids to breakfast." "What brought this on?" she asked with a smile. "Oh, nothing special, it's just been a long time since we spent a Saturday together with the kids. Hey, can we stop at a toy store while we're out? I need to buy some marbles."

The author was inspired by the talk show host. Where will you find your *inspiration*? How will you respond when you encounter that inspiring moment? Will you be momentarily moved or will it permanently influence your daily interactions and purpose?

Family, I encourage you to find the things that permanently light your fire so that you will never have to be inspired again.

"Your work is going to fill a large part of your life, and the only way to be truly satisfied is to do what you believe is great work. And the only way to do great work is to love what you do. If you haven't found it yet, keep looking. Don't settle. As with all matters of the heart, you'll know when you find it."
Steve Jobs

"I hate every minute of training, but I said 'Don't quit. Suffer now and live the rest of your life as a champion." Muhammad Ali

"I dream my painting and I paint my dream" Vincent van Gogh

J

Joy
1: a state of happiness or felicity; bliss

John 15:11 (ESV)

11 These things I have spoken to you, that my joy may be in you, and that your joy may be full.

In this verse we see that if we can stay in God's presence we will find *joy*. If you're doing something without joy, then why do it? *Joy* is an emotion that propels us to greatness. I don't want anybody preparing something for me without *joy*.

As I grew older, my mother would often call my family to come over to her house when she was cooking. It didn't matter what we were doing; my wife would stop and say, "Let's go eat". We understood that my mother was not just cooking a meal to feed our appetite. Being able to serve us brought my mother a feeling of *joy*.

The time we spent with my mother as a family not only filled me physically, but it filled me emotionally as well.

Make sure that you are surrounded by people that do all things with _joy_. People with true _joy_ exude an aura that can be felt in their actions and words. _Joy_ creates an atmosphere of happiness. _Joy_ is appreciating what you have, even when you desire there to be more.

There's a sentimental story that encapsulates the feelings of _joy_ and understanding that _joy_ itself is enough.

I Wish You Enough

At an airport I overheard a mother and daughter in their last moments together. They had announced her plane's departure and standing near the door, she said to her daughter, "I love you, I wish you enough." She said, "Mom, our life together has been more than enough. Your love is all I ever needed. I wish you enough, too, Mom."

They kissed good-bye and she left. She walked over toward the window where I was seated.

Standing there I could see she wanted and needed to cry. I tried not to intrude on her privacy, but she welcomed me in by asking, "Did you ever say good-bye to someone knowing it would be forever?"

"Yes, I have," I replied. Saying that brought back memories I had of expressing my love and appreciation for all my Mom had done for me. Recognizing that her days were limited, I took the time to tell her face to face how much she meant to me. So I knew what this woman was experiencing.

"Forgive me for asking, but why is this a forever good-bye?" I asked.
"I am old and she lives much too far away. I have challenges ahead and the reality is, her next trip back will be for my funeral," she said.
"When you were saying good-bye I heard you say, 'I wish you enough.' May I ask what that means?" She began to smile. "That's a wish that has been handed down from other generations. My parents used to say it to everyone."

She paused for a moment and looking up as if trying to remember it in detail, she smiled even more. "When we said 'I wish you enough,' we were wanting the other person to have a life filled with enough good things to sustain them," she continued and then turning toward me she shared the following as if she were reciting it from memory.

"I wish you enough sun to keep your attitude bright.
I wish you enough rain to appreciate the sun more.
I wish you enough happiness to keep your spirit alive.
I wish you enough pain so that the smallest joys in life appear much bigger.
I wish you enough gain to satisfy your wanting.
I wish you enough loss to appreciate all that you possess.
I wish enough "Hello's" to get you through the final "Good-bye."

Despite the mother knowing she was saying good bye for the final time, she found _joy_ in knowing that her daughter had enough of everything she needed to be great.

Often times we get so overwhelmed by focusing on how bad it is, that we can't find _joy_. Thank goodness we have reminders that can show us that it could be worse.

In Budapest, a man went to a rabbi and complained, saying, "Life is unbearable. There are nine of us living in one room. What can I do?" The rabbi answered, saying, "Take your goat into the room with you." The man was incredulous at first, but the rabbi insisted, assuring the man, saying, "Do as I say and come back in a week." A week later the man came back, looking even more distraught than before. He told the rabbi, "We can't stand it. The goat is filthy." So, the rabbi told him then, "Go home and let the goat out, then come back in a week."

A week later the man returned, radiant. He told the rabbi, "Life is beautiful. We enjoy every minute of it now that there's no goat, only the nine of us!"

Family, let's remember that we may not be where we want to be, but we are far away from where we used to be. Let us find _joy_ in the journey that we have traveled.

Every dark cloud has given us strength we need to overcome and for that reason alone, we should have _joy_.

"Focus on the journey, not the destination. Joy is found not in finishing an activity but in doing it." Greg Anderson

"Joy is prayer; joy is strength: joy is love; joy is a net of love by which you can catch souls." Mother Teresa

"Worry never robs tomorrow of its sorrow, it only saps today of its joy." Leo Buscaglia

"Joy is the simplest form of gratitude." Karl Barth

K

Knowledge

1: the fact or condition of knowing something with familiarity gained through experience or association
2: acquaintance with or understanding of a science, art, or technique

Proverbs 18:15 (AMP)

15 The mind of the prudent is ever getting knowledge, and the ear of the wise is ever seeking (inquiring for and craving) knowledge.

This verse is a reminder that we must always seek to learn, to reflect on the past and to seek *knowledge* for the future. Our life is based on choices, decisions, and consequences we have made along the way. The choices that we have made in the past are responsible for our current place. I have learned that we can only make good decisions based on having good information.

The process of consistently gathering information is how we acquire *knowledge*.

Our *knowledge* base is determined by the voices and choices we utilize on our journey. Most of us have a GPS system in our cars or on our phones. Because of its availability we become comfortable listening to the voice; allowing it to direct us towards our destination. If the GPS is reliable, it increases our comfort level in the voice as we follow its directions. We qualify the voice to be knowledgeable. It's our responsibility to also qualify the voices we allow to speak into our lives on a daily basis. You are where you are in life based on the voices that you have qualified and the choices you make based on the recommendations of those voices.

Knowledge also comes by relying on those who may know more than you to get understanding. I read this story that describes the true value of *knowledge*.

A giant ship engine failed. The ship's owners tried one expert engine. Then they brought in an old man who had been fixing ships since he was a young man. He carried a large bag of tools with him, and when he arrived, he immediately went to work. He inspected the engine very carefully from top to bottom.

Two of the ship's owners were there, watching this man, hoping he would know what to do. After looking things over, the old man reached into his bag and pulled out a small hammer. He gently tapped something. Instantly, the engine lurched into life. He carefully put his hammer away. The engine was fixed! A week later, the owners received a bill from the old man for ten thousand dollars.

"What?!" the owners exclaimed. "He hardly did anything!"
So they wrote the old man a note saying, "Please send us an itemized bill."
The man sent a bill that read:
Tapping with a hammer... ... ... $ 2.00
Knowing where to tap... ... ... $ 9,998.00

You see family, the man was able to charge as he saw fit, because he had more <u>knowledge</u> than the ship owners.

Effort is important, but knowing where to make an effort makes all the difference! Keep studying hard. Don't give up!
Author Unknown

Our quest for _knowledge_ should never diminish for there is so much that we do not know. We should leave more space in our brain for the unknown than the known. Acquiring _knowledge_ can often be scary for it will take us out of our comfort zone.

I can attest to this first hand; my IT team has been pushing me to grab a hold of all the new technology available. My IT team believes all of the new technology would save time and money for our organization. I have been apprehensive because of my fear of the unknown. Once I got over myself, my apprehension and identified that I was the problem, I arranged for them to provide me with private tutoring. Yes, I am completely out of my comfort zone with all of this new technology, but my lack of _knowledge_ will not be the reason that we don't grow.

Question: Is your lack of _knowledge_ holding you back from the success that God has called you to today?

Hosea 4:6 (NIV)

6 my people are destroyed from lack of knowledge. "Because you have rejected knowledge, I also reject you as my priests; because you have ignored the law of your God, I also will ignore your children.

Knowledge isn't based on the number of degrees that a person holds. A person can have a Ph.D. and still not have the desires of their heart. _Knowledge_ is only truly gained by living the word of God. Free yourself from the opinions of others.

The bible is filled with _knowledge_ and God is waiting for you to apply it to your life. From the moment that you confess to learn from Him and your actions line up according to His word, then you will experience an abundance of blessings.

L

Listen

1: to give ear to: hear
2: to hear something with thoughtful attention: give consideration <*listen* to a plea>

Proverbs 1:5 (AMP)

5 The wise also will hear and increase in learning, and the person of understanding will acquire skill and attain to sound counsel [so that he may be able to steer his course rightly]

This scripture says it best; you will ultimately live on the level of your *listening*. The better your *listening* skills are developed the better your opportunity for success. No one wants to repeat themselves, but sadly we often have to because people fail to *listen*.

Question: How is your listening?

Listening is a skill that must be developed over time. We cannot allow our past experiences to clutter our *listening* filter.

We must learn how to *listen* to first understand the speaker and not to respond.

"The Lighthouse Joke"

Believe it or not...this is the transcript of an actual radio conversation between a US naval ship and Canadian authorities off the coast of Newfoundland in October 1995. The Radio conversation was released by the Chief of Naval Operations on Oct. 10, 1995.

US Ship: Please divert your course 0.5 degrees to the south to avoid a collision.

*CND reply: Recommend you divert **your** course 15 degrees to the South to avoid a collision.*

*US Ship: This is the Captain of a US Navy Ship. I say again, divert **your** course.*

CND reply: No. I say again, you divert YOUR course!

US Ship: THIS IS THE AIRCRAFT CARRIER USS CORAL SEA; WE ARE A LARGE WARSHIP OF THE US NAVY. DIVERT YOUR COURSE NOW!!

CND reply: This is a lighthouse; your call.

Question: Are you listening or are you responding?

"God gave us two ears and one mouth, so we ought to listen twice as much as we speak."
Irish Proverb

To sit and actively *listen* can often be tough. There are several components that demonstrate active *listening*. One of the components is the ability to let your speaker finish their complete thought. The body language that you display when the person is speaking also demonstrates that you are *listening*. For instance, you should always face the speaker and maintain eye contact. Your posture should be attentive, but relaxed. Leaning in demonstrates that you care about what is being said and that you respect the person who is speaking. Allow the speaker to speak without interruption, and ask clarifying questions only after the speaker has completed their full thought. When it is time for you to speak, paraphrase what was heard. Asking questions will provide clarity and will demonstrate the value you place on the conversation.

Although the words we say carry weight, it is often what is unsaid that holds more weight. In fact, 55% of our communication is non-verbal.

"One of the most sincere forms of respect is actually listening to what another has to say."
Bryant H. McGill

M

Motivate

1: the act or process of giving someone a reason for doing something: the act or process of motivating someone
2: the condition of being eager to act or work: the condition of being motivated
3: a force or influence that causes someone to do something

Hebrews 10:24 (NLT)

24 Let us think of ways to motivate one another to acts of love and good works.

The path our life takes is often the source of our *motivation*. I had the opportunity to play in the NFL on the brightest stage of life. I also had the opportunity to work in Walmart (not disparaging either). In both situations, I realized what separated people the most was their ability to stay *motivated*.

In my opinion, there is nothing worse in life than wanting something for someone else more than they want it for themselves.

I have learned it is extremely hard to _motivate_ the unmotivated. People are where they are for a reason. I repeat -- people are where they are for a reason. So stop trying to turn people into who you want them to be. You can't _motivate_ the unmotivated. You are better off finding someone who is self-motivated and helping to direct their energy into a positive future.

If you want to be successful, you must stay _motivated_. _Motivation_ is much like food; without it you cannot survive. We will all have our different trials and tribulations that we must endure. _Motivation_ is the key to propelling yourself past temporary setbacks. Walmart was not in my plans, it was a temporary setback, but I was _motivated_ to not allow it to become a permanent setback.

The word _motivation_ comes from the Latin verb _movere_, meaning to move. There are two types of _motivation_ — extrinsic and intrinsic.

Extrinsic _motivation_ is based on an external

reward that you will get once the task is completed. On the other spectrum, there is intrinsic _motivation_; which is based on the idea that the activity itself is the reward. Thus, when you are intrinsically motivated, you do what you do because you enjoy it and not because someone told you to do it or because you will get a reward as a result.

Steve Jobs was well-known in the technology world. Jobs overcame several obstacles only to be faced with imminent sickness at the height of his success. Threatened by the thought of being replaced, Jobs became intrinsically motivated to get better and to do something that he loved -- design. This time Jobs wasn't designing a new iPhone; rather, he designed a boat.

"I didn't think I would be alive when it got done, but that made me so sad, and I decided that working on the design was fun to do, and maybe I have a shot at being alive when it's done. If I stop work on the boat and then I make it alive for another two years, I would be really pissed. So I've kept going."
Steve Jobs

Steve Jobs passed before the construction of the boat was completed. But I think it's safe to say that he felt motivated to the very end.

"Wanting something is not enough. You must hunger for it. Your motivation must be absolutely compelling in order to overcome the obstacles that will invariably come your way." Les Brown

Question: What is your *motivation*?

Motivation is a driving force that will push us past whatever obstacles life will throw our way. We must be driven by intrinsic *motivation*; for if our actions themselves are the reward, then we will take pride in every action and complete with excellence.

N

Navigate

1: To find the way to get to a place when you are traveling in a ship, airplane, car, etc.

Psalm 32:8(NLT)

8 The Lord says, "I will guide you along the best pathway for your life. I will advise you and watch over you.

Because of self-will, we can choose the path in life that we want to take. However, this passage says that God is there to *navigate* us. Our Plan B is often God's Plan A, for He already knows the pathway that will lead us to the most success. Often times that pathway is covered in potholes and traffic, so we turn the cruise control off and decide to *navigate* ourselves.

We all have the challenge of navigating through life. It would be so much easier if life was a nicely paved street with no curved roads. Life would be easier if we already knew our destination.

I know for me, I never in a million years would have believed that I would be a pastor. But God changed my course as He has done with many of us. Our ability to _navigate_ "should" improve as we get older. I say "should" improve, because some people go through the trial repeatedly and never learn the lesson; thus they never improve. We must learn from our past mistakes to improve our current direction in life.

When I was ten years old my mother was in a horrific car accident that should have killed us, but God said differently. A driver crossed over the median and we were crushed into a concrete barrier. My mother developed a driving phobia as a result of the accident. My mother's method of navigating her phobia was to then teach me how to drive and I became her personal chauffer. My mother would task me with the duty of picking up people from all over the Washington, DC area.

People would ask how I knew how to get to certain places and my mother would say, "Jomo has been driving for a long time".

We should all become navigators over time. All of life's u-turns and wrong turns have provided us with learning experiences. Now, I may be a bit presumptuous here, but only a fool continues to repeat the same mistakes.

> *"The best way to navigate through life is to give up all of our controls."*
> *Gerald Jampolsky*

> *"I've been able to stay good because of my family and keeping God first. If you don't have God in your life, how are you going to navigate through this world?" Keke Palmer*

Change begins with you. If you want something different you must be willing to do something different. You must be willing to change your path and to *navigate* to a detour that will provide a different outcome.

You must be willing to *navigate* past your will and follow God's will and ways.

O

Opportunity

1: an amount of time or a situation in which something can be done

Ephesians 5:16 (AMP)

16 Making the very most of the time [buying up each opportunity], because the days are evil.

An *opportunity* is a window of time that has the ability to constantly open and close. The success of our lives will be determined by the windows we chose to jump through when they are open. The greatest challenge in life is not having the ability to jump; rather it is recognizing when to jump out of the window.

I have learned that sometimes God will have you jump out of the window before you think you're ready. Oftentimes, by the time we are ready to jump, the window has already closed. Sometimes we aren't ready to jump because we fear the obstacles in our way. We fear what waits for us once we jump.

*I read this great story about obstacles,
In ancient times, a King had a boulder placed
on a roadway. Then he hid himself and
watched to see if anyone would remove the
huge rock. Some of the King's' wealthiest
merchants and courtiers came by and simply
walked around it. Many loudly blamed the
King for not keeping the roads clear, but none
did anything about getting the stone out of the
way. Then a peasant came along carrying a
load of vegetables. Upon approaching the
boulder, the peasant laid down his burden
and tried to move the stone to the side of the
road. After much pushing and straining, he
finally succeeded. After the peasant picked up
his load of vegetables, he noticed a purse
lying in the road where the boulder had been.
The purse contained many gold coins and a
note from the King indicating that the gold
was for the person who removed the boulder
from the roadway.*

In this story, the peasant learned what many
of us never understand; every obstacle
presents an *opportunity* to grow! Each time
we move past an obstacle, we show God that
we believe in His Word.

We have to make a choice to act on the _opportunity_ or to turn around in fear. The time period given to make that choice is not always as long as we hope. We must prove that we are walking by faith and not by sight.

In this life we will all face obstacles and it's critical that we don't turn our obstacles into mountains.

"Never lose an opportunity of seeing anything beautiful, for beauty is God's handwriting."
Ralph Waldo Emerson

"If a window of opportunity appears, don't pull down the shade." Tom Peters

Matthew 17:20 (AMP)

20 He answered, "Because of your little faith [your lack of trust and confidence in the power of God]; for I assure you and most solemnly say to you, [a]if you have [living] faith the size of a mustard seed, you will say to this mountain, 'Move from here to there,' and [if it is God's will] it will move; and nothing will be impossible for you.

Jesus is telling us to speak to our obstacles. I don't know what obstacles you may be facing today, but I know you cannot allow your obstacles to talk to you. I have learned that the best way to predict your future is to speak it into existence.

We must not focus on our obstacles we must focus on our God. Our God is bigger than any obstacle you will ever face. Some of my greatest blessings were masked as obstacles. So don't focus on the obstacle, focus on the *opportunity*. Winning in life is all about maximizing your opportunities.

"Opportunity often comes disguised in the form of misfortune, or temporary defeat."
Napoleon Hill

P

Purpose
1: the reason why something is done or used: the aim or intention of something
2: the feeling of being determined to do or achieve something
3: the aim or goal of a person: what a person is trying to do, become, etc.

1 Kings 5:5(AMPC)

5 And I purpose to build a house to the Name of the Lord my God, as the Lord said to David my father, Your son whom I will set on your throne in your place shall build the house to My Name and Presence.

In this verse we see Solomon's *purpose* was to fulfill the goal of his father King David in building a temple for the Lord. This *purpose* became the driving force of all his goals. Clarified *purpose* will crystalize goals.
Our existence was not an accident. We were made on *purpose* and for a *purpose*.

Until you're walking in your *purpose* you will never fulfill the call on your life.

What is driving you? What is pushing you? Why do you get up in the morning? _Purpose_!

In everything there is a _purpose_. Even if you are in pain and hurting mentally, physically, or emotionally, you can find _purpose_ in your pain. When you find the _purpose_ of that pain you will find power; power to propel into deeper _purpose_.

Question: Why do you do what you do?

If you can answer that question, you will nail down your _purpose_. _Purpose_ is critical as it provides direction. It helps you maintain focus on your goals and stay motivated to achieve them.

I love this story of a frustrated young man who went to see the wise man in his village.

"I don't know what to do with my life. How do I find my purpose?" the young man asked.
"Follow me," said the old man.
Silently, they trudged together to a faraway river where they found dozens of prospectors panning for gold.
"There are three types of prospectors here," the sage said.

"What do you mean?" the young man inquired.

"There are those who strike gold straight away. Excited, they take their plunder, cash it in and live comfortably for the rest of their lives. Then there are those who pan for years. They know that there is gold here and they have seen others strike it rich, so they persist until they too find the gold that they've been searching for."

"What about the third type?" asked the young man.

"They are the individuals who get frustrated that they haven't found what they are looking for, so after a day, a week or a year or more, they give up, walk away and never find gold."

Slightly confused, the young man asked, "What has this got to do with finding my purpose?"

"Aah yes, the age-old question." the old man smiled and looked his companion in the eye.

"There are those in life who look for their purpose and seem to find it almost immediately. From a young age they have a clear sense of purpose and pursue their dreams with energy and enthusiasm.

Some others have to look a bit harder, perhaps for many years, but if they persist and keep looking, they will find something to live for. Finally, there are those who want to know their purpose, but they become frustrated with the search and give up too soon, returning to a life of meaningless wandering."

"Can everyone find their purpose?"

"Is there gold in the river?" the wise man responded.

"So, how do I find my own purpose?"

"Keep looking."

"But what if I want to find it quicker?"

"Son, there are no guarantees that you will be able to find it quickly, the only guarantee is that if you give up and stop looking for it, you'll never find it."

The young man looked despondent, feeling that he had wasted his time with the old man.

He felt a reassuring hand on his shoulder, "I can sense your frustration, but let me assure you, if you can find your true calling in life, you will live with passion, make the world a better place, be richer than you could imagine and feel as though the very face of God Himself is smiling upon you.

That may happen next week, next year or in the years ahead, but the search will be worth it and your life will never be the same again. So for now, your purpose is to find your purpose."

"Thanks."

"Oh, and there's one other thing that I forgot to mention."

"What's that?"

"Just as those men and women need to get down to the river with a pan to find their gold, so we need to remain active to find our purposes, we don't find it sitting around at home doing nothing."

It was getting late, so the two men turned for home and began their long walk back to the village.

As they walked, the young man was deep in thought about what he had just learned, and the wise man smiled to himself, knowing that conversations like this were an important part of living his own purpose.

So often we are like this young man; we want the immediate answer and God tells us to be patient, keep looking, keep searching, it is within your reach.

Question: Do you know your *purpose*? Are you still looking? Or have you given up?

"Learn to get in touch with the silence within yourself, and know that everything in life has purpose. There are no mistakes, no coincidences, all events are blessings given to us to learn from." Elisabeth Kubler-Ross

Family, some of you are already living in your *purpose*, yet you are still searching. Be still, be prayerful and know that you are destined to walk in your *purpose*.

Q

Question

1: an act or instance of asking

1 Corinthians 2:15(AMPC)

15 But the spiritual man tries all things [he examines, investigates, inquires into, questions, and discerns all things], yet is himself to be put on trial and judged by no one [he can read the meaning of everything, but no one can properly discern or appraise or get an insight into him].

There is so much about life that is unknown that it should entice you to ask *questions*. In this verse we see that a spiritual man asks many *questions*. *Questions* bring clarity, peace, and help create a sense of certainty. If you don't know something, you need to ask!

This verse in James confirms that God wants us to ask Him questions.

James 1:5 Amplified Bible (AMP)

5 If any of you lacks wisdom [to guide him through a decision or circumstance], he is to ask of [our benevolent] God, who gives to everyone generously and without rebuke or blame, and it will be given to him.

This verse is such an encouragement to me, because who knows more about our situations than God and God is giving us permission to ask Him.

Question: Who do you seek your knowledge from?

Do you go to your friends, spouse, or co-workers? Family, we have to get in the habit of asking God first. I am not saying not to ask these people, but I am telling you that I have learned to ask God first because He already has the answers.

"Leaders who ask, listen, learn and consistently follow up are seen as becoming more effective. Leaders, who don't ask, don't get much better." Howard Morgan

This quote reminds me of an article I read about managers and the questions they ask.

I recently asked the vice president of customer satisfaction in a major organization if his employees should be asking their key customers for feedback - listening, learning and following up to ensure service keeps getting better. "Of course," he replied. "How important it this to your company?" I asked. "It's damn important!" he exclaimed. I then lowered my voice and asked, "Have you ever asked your wife for feedback on how you can become a better husband?" He stopped, thought for a second, and sighed, "No." "Who is more important - your company's customers or your wife?" I asked. "My wife, of course," he replied. "If you believe in asking so much, why don't you do it at home?" I inquired. He ruefully admitted, "Because I am afraid of the answer."

I challenge you to step past your fears. Ask God the hard questions. Often the answer is something we don't want to hear, but need to hear.

"I never learn anything talking. I only learn things when I ask questions." Lou Holtz

I said it before and I will say it again, there is so much about life that is unknown. I challenge you to learn more today than you did yesterday. Share your knowledge, do not judge when others ask you questions.

Question: What is the first *question* you are going to ask?

R

Respect

1: a feeling or understanding that someone or something is important, serious, etc., and should be treated in an appropriate way

1 Peter 2:17 (NLT)

17 Respect everyone, and love the family of believers. [a] Fear God, and respect the king.

The scripture leaves no room for confusion; everyone deserves respect. God is the only one that should be both feared and respected. My mother taught me to *respect* people in the manner in which she lived. I have learned that whom you do not *respect*, you do not honor. If you do not honor a person, you also cannot receive their contribution. We can learn from anybody, so we should *respect* everybody.

Respect is given as an act of worship to God the Father. Another word for *respect* is honor. When we give honor we are displaying preferential treatment to someone or something.

We give _respect_ not because of how we are treated; rather we give _respect_ because of who we represent.

Respect should be given at all times; you never know when you may need someone's assistance. Take the story of two princes for example.

Once upon a time, the King's two young princes were playing in a forest, and - meeting one at a time, they came across four dwarves who asked them to be more careful. The first dwarf had a headache and he asked them not to shout. The second dwarf was painting a landscape, and he asked the children to move away because they were blocking out the light. The third dwarf was doing a giant jigsaw puzzle in the middle of the road, and he asked the children not to tread on it. The fourth dwarf was watching a butterfly and he asked them not to frighten it away.

One young prince who respected others did as the dwarves asked, but the other young prince ignored the dwarves' pleas, and kept bothering them. In the evening, both boys had become separated and lost.

*They needed to get back to the palace quickly.
Each of them separately came across the four
dwarves again, and asked for their help. They
refused to help the disrespectful prince, but
with the respectful prince they did whatever
they could to help, and took him along some
secret tracks which led right to the palace.
The other prince arrived much later, and was
punished for it. He now understood that it's
much better to respect everyone if you want to
have friends.*

The moral of the story…you never know
when you may need directions. Seriously
family, <u>*respect*</u> is received to those who have
given respect. Remember, you reap what you
sow. <u>*Respect*</u> is one of the easiest things to
sow and it is also one of the most powerful
indications of a person's character.

*"I firmly believe that respect is a lot more
important, and a lot greater, than
popularity." Julius Erving*

*"We should all consider each other as human
beings, and we should respect each other."
Malala Yousafzai*

"I'm not concerned with your liking or disliking me…All I ask is that you respect me as a human being." Jackie Robinson

I read a great story of a few men who were in a foreign land for an extended stay. As part of their stay, the company provided them a home to stay and a cook to help them. The men got bored in their down time and started playing practical jokes on each other. The practical jokes then turned to the cook. They would booby trap doors with water buckets that would fall on his head. They would make jokes about his accent. They would lock him out at times, all in the name of fun. The cook just went along knowing his job was to serve them and he needed the money. The time eventually came for the men to go home. They would no longer have the opportunity to make a joke out of the cook. They wanted to apologize and they did. The cook responded with his own apology for spitting in their food every time they played a joke on him.

The moral of the story is that everyone deserves _respect_ and we have a moral obligation to give it. Though the men believed they were being funny, the cook received it as disrespect.

As a result, he disrespected them on a different level.

Family, I say again, you reap what you sow; our everyday words and actions have long standing effects. I'm reminded of a story of a young boy who was taught a tough lesson about respect.

A long time ago there was a boy. He was smart, talented and handsome. However, he was very selfish and his temper was so difficult, that nobody wanted to be friends with him. Often he got angry and said various hurtful things to people around him.

The boy's parents were very concerned about his bad temper. They considered what they could do and one day the father had an idea. He called his son and gave him a hammer and a bag of nails. The father said: "Every time you get angry, take a nail and drive it into that old fence as hard as you can."
The fence was very tough and the hammer was heavy, nevertheless the boy was so furious that during the very first day he had driven 37 nails.
Day after day, week after week, the number of nails was gradually decreasing.

After some time, the boy started to understand that holding his temper is easier that driving nails into the fence.

One day the boy didn't need the hammer and nails anymore as he learned to hold his temper perfectly. So he came to his father and told him about his achievement. "Now, every time you hold your temper all day long, pull out one nail".

Much time passed. At last the boy could be proud of himself as all the nails were gone. When he went to his father and told him about this, he offered to come and take a careful look at the fence. "You did a good job, my son, though pay your attention to the holes that are left from the nails.

The fence will never be the same. The same happens when you say hurtful things to people, as your words leave scars in their hearts like those holes in the fence.

Remember, we need to treat everyone with love and respect, because it doesn't matter, that you say you are sorry, the scars will not disappear."

I challenge you to ensure that each day you treat everyone you meet with _respect_. You treat them with kindness, despite how they may treat you.

You never know who is watching and you want to be sure they are seeing the best you possible.

"Be kind, don't judge, and have respect for others. If we can all do this, the world would be a better place. The point is to teach this to the next generation." Jasmine Guinness

S

Success

1: the fact of getting or achieving wealth, respect, or fame
2: the correct or desired result of an attempt
3: someone or something that is successful: a person or thing that succeeds

Joshua 1:8 (AMPC)

8 This Book of the Law shall not depart out of your mouth, but you shall meditate on it day and night, that you may observe and do according to all that is written in it. For then you shall make your way prosperous, and then you shall deal wisely and have good [b]success.

I love how this verse makes it clear that _success_ is a choice. People often believe that _success_ is a byproduct of certain affiliations, family lineage, education, or who you may know.

This verse makes it clear that knowledge of God's word and obedience to it will be the pathway to your _success_.

Success leaves clues. Notice how the verse states "you shall make your way prosperous, and then you shall deal wisely and have good success", we have a direct impact on our level of _success_. With _success_ not just dealing with money, but an environment where we have nothing missing and nothing lacking.

As a former business coach and life strategist this is a topic near and dear to my heart. Before you can delve into this word we must not only define it, but we must understand what _success_ looks like. I see many people who are searching for something they have not yet defined. Everyone's definition of _success_ is different.

 For some it means a paid off home, the promotion you have been seeking, marriage, your kid's graduation, or the body you have dreamed of and the list goes on and on. It is impossible to fulfill what you have not defined. Defining what _success_ means to you personally is your responsibility.

"If you carefully consider what you want to be said of you in the funeral experience, you will find your definition of success."
Stephen Covey

When you reach a point in your life when you feel successful, you will also feel relieved. Walking in God's purpose leads you towards *success*, because that is God's plan for your life. You are destined to have *success*, destined for greatness, destined to be at peace.

My definition of *success* is the state of being where you have a full grasp of your formula to attain your goals. Simply put, you have identified the keys that you can duplicate in any environment to give you the desired result. I remember when I travelled the country, training people on *success*. I knew that if I had twelve to fifteen events in a month that I would have a successful month. I also knew that if we had less than that, we would be in trouble. We knew our numbers and keys to our *success*. You must take some time out and study your life patterns to identify what it will take for you to achieve the *success* you desire. *Success* is fulfilled by planning and will never be fulfilled where no plan exists.

"Success is peace of mind, which is a direct result of self-satisfaction in knowing you did your best to become the best you are capable of becoming," John Wooden

"Success is liking yourself, liking what you do, and liking how you do it." Maya Angelou

Your idea of <u>success</u> is almost certainly different from the next person. Do not define your <u>success</u> based on other's opinions. <u>Success</u> is yours to have, but you must want it more than anything else.

"Success is 1% inspiration, 99% perspiration." Thomas Edison

Each day when you wake, fight for your peace of mind, fight for your satisfaction, enjoy the process and never give up. For each day leads you one step closer to <u>success</u>.

In my journey of life, I have identified a few tips to success that I want to share:

The price of <u>success</u> is paid for in advance.

People often want <u>success</u> without paying the cost for <u>success</u>. There is a price for <u>success</u> that often comes with sacrifice, discipline and commitment that will often separate the successful from the unsuccessful.

There is no financing of _success_, in our world of financing where everything can be received now and paid for it later. You will not achieve _success_ in life without paying the price.

> *"The dictionary is the only place where success comes before work" Vince Lombardi*

The price remains the same.

People are often trying to find a way to achieve _success_ at a discounted price. Listen family, there are no sales when it comes to _success_. It is always available, but there aren't many people who will press through the adversities that life will throw at you to attain it. _Success_ is always in vogue, it never goes out of style and is always in demand.

> *"Success is going from failure to failure without losing enthusiasm."*
> *Winston Churchill*

The price only increases in value; it's an asset and not a liability.

Success is always for sale and never out of stock, but very few are willing to pay that price.

Success is in great supply but few demand it of themselves. _Success_ is no respecter of person. _Success_ doesn't discriminate, it only elevates. _Success_ just wants to be utilized.

> *"Defeat is not the worst of failures. Not to have tried is the true failure."*
> *George Edward Woodberry*

T

Trust

1: firm belief in the reliability, truth, ability, or strength of someone or something.

Proverbs 3:5 (AMP)

5 Lean on, trust in, and be confident in the Lord with all your heart and mind and do not rely on your own insight or understanding.

The amount of success in your life is impacted by the voices that we choose to *trust* enough to speak into our lives. We have all seen that cartoon with the good angel and the bad angel and both are speaking to the character at the same time.

We must *trust* our inner voice; if you are saved I am speaking of the Holy Spirit. We must develop an inner *trust* and an outer *trust*. Inner *trust* deals with our relationship with our maker and the third part of the Trinity, The Holy Spirit.

We must also develop or cultivate a dream team, outer _trust_, of people that are allowed to speak into our lives when we a veering off course.

We must _trust_ our inner voice. You demonstrate your level of _trust_ in God by the level of your faith. Your faith, your belief and your _trust_ are one in the same.

The amazing story of Charles Blondin, a famous French tightrope walker, is a wonderful illustration of what true faith is.

Blondin's greatest fame came on September 14, 1860, when he became the first person to cross a tightrope stretched 11,000 feet (over a quarter of a mile) across the mighty Niagara Falls. People from both Canada and America came from miles away to see this great feat. He walked across, 160 feet above the falls, several times... each time with a different daring feat - once in a sack, on stilts, on a bicycle, in the dark, and blindfolded. One time he even carried a stove and cooked an omelet in the middle of the rope!

A large crowd gathered and the buzz of excitement ran along both sides of the river bank.

The crowd "Oohed and Aahed!" as Blondin carefully walked across - one dangerous step after another –

pushing a wheelbarrow holding a sack of potatoes.

Then a one point, he asked for the participation of a volunteer. Upon reaching the other side, the crowd's applause was louder than the roar of the falls!

Blondin suddenly stopped and addressed his audience: "Do you believe I can carry a person across in this wheelbarrow?"

The crowd enthusiastically yelled, "Yes! You are the greatest tightrope walker in the world. We believe!"

"Okay," said Blondin, "Who wants to get into the wheelbarrow." As far as the Blondin story goes, no one did at the time!

This unique story illustrates a real life picture of faith in action looks like. The crowd watched these daring feats. They said they believed in Blondin, but their actions proved they truly did not believe.

Similarly, it is one thing for us to say we believe in God.

However, what is our response when we are asked to step out on a tight rope? Do we _trust_ our faith in God's abilities to protect us and guide us safely to the other side?

Family, it is sometimes easier said than done, but true faith is when we believe God and put our faith and _trust_ in His Son, Jesus Christ.

A man just got married and was returning home with his wife. They were crossing a lake in a boat, when suddenly a great storm arose. The man was a warrior, but the woman became very much afraid because it seemed almost hopeless.
The boat was small and the storm was really huge and at any moment they were going to be drowned. But the man sat silently, calm and quiet, as if nothing was happening. The woman was trembling and she said, "Are you not afraid? This may be our last moment of life! It doesn't seem that we will be able to reach the other shore. Only some miracle can save us; otherwise death is certain. Are you not afraid? Are you mad or something? Are you a stone or something?"

The man laughed and took the sword out of its sheath. The woman was even more puzzled: What was he doing? Then he brought the naked sword close to the woman's neck, so close that just a small gap was there, it was almost touching her neck.

He said, "Are you afraid?"

She started to laugh and said,

"Why should I be afraid? If the sword is in your hands, why I should be afraid? I know you love me."

He put the sword back and said, "This is my answer. I know God Loves me, and the storm is in His hand. So whatsoever is going to happen is going to be good. If we survive, good; if we don't survive, good because everything is in His hands and He cannot do anything wrong."

The moral of this story – develop *trust*. This is the *trust* which one needs to embody and which is capable of transforming your whole life. Any less won't do!

"Trust is the glue of life. It's the most essential ingredient in effective communication. It's the foundational principle that holds all relationships." Stephen Covey

"...You say to God, 'I have never seen you provide for me.' God says to you, 'You have never trusted me." Corallie Buchanan

U

Unique

1: being the only one of its kind; unlike anything else.

Jeremiah 1:5 (ESV)

"Before I formed you in the womb I knew you, and before you were born I consecrated you; I appointed you a prophet to the nations."

Psalm 139:14 (ESV)

I praise you, for I am fearfully and wonderfully made. Wonderful are your works; my soul knows it very well.

This scripture is very clear; God knew who we were before we were born. Now, I have started with more scriptures than previous chapters, for it is imperative that you know who you are and your capabilities.

In our society we have so many copycats that we sometimes face temptation to blend in versus being our authentic selves.

Why be a second rate copy when you were intended to be an original?

God has placed wonderful *unique* gifts and talents on the inside of you. Don't be selfish, let your light shine.

> *"The greatness of art is not to find what is common but what is unique."*
> *Isaac Bashevis Singer*

You are fearfully and wonderfully made. You are *unique* and made in God's likeness. When you finally determine what makes you *unique* it is like you have opened a blue Tiffany's box. No two people are made alike, so everyone's *unique* characteristics will look completely different. Your uniqueness may be considered a weakness by some, but you have the ability to make it your strength.

There's a story of one 10-year-old boy who decided to study judo despite the fact that he had lost his left arm in a devastating car accident. The boy began lessons with an old Japanese judo master.

The boy was doing well, so he couldn't understand why, after three months of training the master had taught him only one move. "Sensei," the boy finally asked, "Shouldn't I be learning more moves?" "This is the only move I know, but this is the only move you'll ever need to know," the sensei replied.

Not quite understanding, but believing in his teacher, the boy kept training. Several months later, the sensei took the boy to his first tournament. Surprising himself, the boy easily won his first two matches. The third match proved to be more difficult, but after some time, his opponent became impatient and charged; the boy deftly used his one move to win the match.

Still amazed by his success, the boy was now in the finals. This time, his opponent was bigger, stronger, and more experienced. For a while, the boy appeared to be overmatched. Concerned that the boy might get hurt, the referee called a time-out.

He was about to stop the match when the sensei intervened. "No," the sensei insisted, "Let him continue."

Soon after the match resumed, his opponent made a critical mistake: he dropped his guard. Instantly, the boy used his move to pin him. The boy had won the match and the tournament. He was the champion.

On the way home, the boy and sensei reviewed every move in each and every match. Then the boy summoned the courage to ask what was really on his mind. "Sensei, how did I win the tournament with only one move?" "You won for two reasons," the sensei answered. "First, you've almost mastered one of the most difficult throws in all of judo. And second, the only known defense for that move is for your opponent to grab your left arm."

The boy's biggest weakness had become his biggest strength. In his difference he found his gifting. God has already planted a seed within you that makes you *unique*. You are destined to shine, stand out and leave an impact on the world. There are only two things in this world that are guaranteed, the day we are born and the day that we die.

How will you define the line in between? How will your uniqueness set you apart from everyone else?

Success is based on your ability to capitalize on what makes you *unique*.

"Every man and woman is born into the world to do something unique and something distinctive and if he or she does not do it, it will never be done." Benjamin E. Mays

"Each of you is a unique child of God. God knows you individually. He sends messages of encouragement, correction, and direction fitted to you and to your needs."
Henry B. Eyring

V

Vision

1: the ability to see: sight or eyesight
2: something that you imagine: a picture that you see in your mind

Proverbs 29:18 (NASB)

18 Where there is no vision, the people are unrestrained, but happy is he who keeps the law.

Habakkuk 2 (NKJV)

2 Then the Lord answered me and said: "Write the vision and make it plain on tablets, that he may run who reads it.

The first definition states that *vision* is the ability to see the end; to see past your heartache and pain. *Vision* keeps you focused through life's storms. *Vision* allows you to see past all of the obstacles and trials you have gone through. Every great work started with a *vision*.

To walk in your intended path, you must have the ability to paint the picture on the canvas of your imagination.

When I was growing up, I had a step-brother named John. John was four years older than me and had a dream of being a pilot. We would often go outside and watch planes fly over for fun. John knew the planes so well he could identify the plane by its underbelly. It was not long before I was doing the same thing he was doing; I wanted to be like him. Everyone knew that John wanted to be a pilot. But as life would have it, John couldn't pass the eye test for pilot school and his *vision* of being a pilot died. At least that is what most people thought, but not John.

John worked various jobs along the way, but never gave up the *vision* of being a pilot. Fast forward 15 years and technology has a solution to my brothers' problem -- Lasik eye surgery. The *vision* was delayed not denied. John worked and saved up for pilot school. My brother John is now a pilot for Spirit Airlines. Though his *vision* was blurry for a season, he never lost sight of his *vision*.

What is your response when you encounter an obstacle?

Do you turn and run or keep the faith?
Family, you must push through; keep your
vision on the forefront.

To bring your vision to life, rely on the
scripture. Write your _vision_ down and read it
constantly. Think about Walt Disney, he lost
everything only to focus on his _vision_ of
success.

_Walt Disney was down but not out. It was
1928, and the 26-year-old cartoon animator
was taking the train back to California after a
disastrous trip to New York. His sly
distributor had just taken over the rights to
Disney's first big-time character, Oswald the
Lucky Rabbit, hiring away Disney's best
animators in the process. Although his studio
was left unstaffed and in debt, Disney
wouldn't admit defeat. Instead, he vowed to
start over with what he had - his talent. As the
train shot through the Midwest, Disney
started doodling on a piece of paper. It wasn't
long before Disney thought the doodles
looked like a mouse. "What do you think of
the name Mortimer Mouse?" Disney asked his
wife, Lilly. "Mortimer?" said Lilly, frowning.
"How about Mickey?"_

Disney (1901-66) created Mickey Mouse, the most popular cartoon figure in the world, at a time when his future looked its worst.

Vision enables us to see the invisible; we all have eyes, but that does not mean that we all see. _Vision_ is the ability to form a picture in your mind, to see everything that the future holds for you.

After losing his sight at age 3, Michael May went on to become the first blind CIA agent, set a world record for downhill skiing, and start a successful Silicon Valley company. Then he got the chance to see again.

"Weeks passed. When May mentioned the surgery to people, their responses were predictable and explosive: Sight means you get to see your wife and children; isn't that reason enough? But May didn't conceive of it that way. He felt so fully invested in his family, so in love with them, that he couldn't imagine anything—not even vision— deepening his connection to them.

I already see my wife and kids, he would think to himself.

And he felt that way about much of his life—
that everything already seemed so
wonderfully vivid."

When you have *vision* you can see the end
before you arrive there. You are able to see
past the pain, the trial, the situation and into
the future.

"Have a vision. Be demanding."
Colin Powell

"Where there is no vision, there is no hope."
George Washington Carver

W

Wisdom
1: accumulated philosophic or scientific learning: knowledge
2: ability to discern inner qualities and relationships: insight, good sense
3: judgment

Proverbs 4:7 (AMP)

7 "The beginning of wisdom is: Get [skillful and godly] wisdom [it is preeminent]! And with all your acquiring, get understanding [actively seek spiritual discernment, mature comprehension, and logical interpretation].

You will notice the scripture says in "the beginning", the one thing about _wisdom_ is that it never stops. You will always acquire and accumulate more _wisdom_. You should always want to acquire and accumulate more _wisdom_.

That is why it's so critical to always listen and learn because once you stop listening and learning you stop growing.

You will also notice the scripture says "get", meaning that you have to actively engage in the process of growing in your knowledge. Often when I counsel people and they say that they are no longer connected or see eye-to–eye, it's usually a result of one individual who has stopped growing. There's a great statement that states you are the average of your friends and you will become who you surround yourself with and what you read.

"You are the average of the five people you spend the most time with." Jim Rohn

"Get away from people who have your problem and get around people who have your solution."
Dr. Michael Freeman

Proverbs 11:14 (AMP)

14 Where there is no [wise, intelligent] guidance, the people fall [and go off course like a ship without a helm], But in the abundance of [wise and godly] counselors there is victory.

I love how this scripture points out that we must have *wisdom* to surround ourselves with the right people. A successful person is surrounded by multiple people full of *wisdom*. Each person can have a different area of expertise; this is what helps to build your knowledge portfolio.

We are where we are in life based on the decisions we have made. We can only make good decisions based on the information we have, so our life is all about the accumulation of knowledge. As we gain more knowledge we must have the *wisdom* to make the right decision. People often make the mistake of assuming that just because someone is older than they are that they have *wisdom.* True *wisdom* can be defined as something that is based on consistent decision-making in the right direction.

King Solomon was the wisest man that ever lived and when given the opportunity to ask God for anything he wanted, the one thing he asked for was *wisdom*. He asked for the ability to discern and differentiate between right and wrong so that he could make the proper decision. Our life is often based on the voices we heed and the choices we make.

1 Kings 3:9 (NLT)

9 Give me an understanding heart so that I can govern your people well and know the difference between right and wrong.

We must be mindful of who we fellowship with and what fellows we allow in our ship. You will become who you surround yourself with so choose wisely.

Wisdom is also a defense mechanism. It can shield you from repeating mistakes, been there done that and only a fool continues to make the same mistake.

Ecclesiastes 7:12 (AMP)

12 For wisdom is a protection even as money is a protection, But the [excellent] advantage of knowledge is that wisdom shields and preserves the lives of its possessors.

Proverbs 26:11 (NLT)

11 As a dog returns to its vomit, so a fool repeats his foolishness.

"The definition of insanity is doing the same thing over and over again, but expecting different results." Albert Einstein

There was a time in my life where I would try to convince people of my point of view and would be frustrated when they didn't agree. Then I developed _wisdom_ and realized some would never get it but many would. I have gained _wisdom_ in understanding some battles aren't worth fighting.

In 2015, I was diagnosed with Stage III colon cancer. In the midst of me going through surgery and chemotherapy, my daughter was going through her health challenges and we were trying to build a church. My pastor called me and said he had been praying for my healing of cancer, for my daughter's healing and for the construction of our building. Then the Lord spoke to him and told him to not pray about the building. He said, "Jomo some fights choose you and some fights you choose". He broke it down for me. He said, "Cancer chose you and your daughter's condition chose her, but you are choosing to build a certain way". He then said, "No country can win a battle fighting on every side". It was me.

I was not using wisdom. We must choose our battles wisely. He then said, "Jomo. What's the purpose of getting the building done and you're not there to be in the building?" It was a tough conversation.

Man, he truly deposited some words of <u>wisdom</u> into my life that day. It is not just about getting <u>wisdom</u> that is critical; it is also applying the <u>wisdom</u>.

Many times <u>wisdom</u> will force you to make tough decisions.

"By three methods we may learn wisdom: First, by reflection, which is noblest; second, by imitation, which is easiest; and third by experience, which is the bitterest." Confucius

X

X = Time

1: the measured or measurable period during which an action, process, or condition exists or continues

2 Corinthians 6:2 (AMP)

2 for He says, "at the acceptable time I listened to you, and on the salvation I helped you." Behold, now is the day of salvation

Ecclesiastes 3:1-8 (AMP)

1 There is a season (a time appointed) for everything and a time for every delight and event or purpose under heaven.

In math, X is used to represent the unknown; something that we know will occur but we are not sure when. *Time* is a variable that is both known and unknown.

The scripture points out that God has a determined time for our existence and when we have completed our purpose, we will arrive at salvation. This confirms that *time* cannot be controlled; it can only be managed.

People who understand how to properly manage their *time* are more productive. We all have the same 24 hours in a day; however, there is a difference in how we manage our *time*. We can always make more money, but you cannot make more *time*. This is why we need to place a premium on our *time*.

Imagine there is a bank that credits your account each morning with $86,400. It carries over no balance from day to day. Every evening deletes whatever part of the balance you failed to use during the day.

What would you do? Draw out every cent, of course!

Each of us has such a bank; its name is *time*. Every morning, it credits you with 86,400 seconds. Every night, the amount that you fail to invest is erased. *Time* does not allow us to carry a balance into the next day. *Time* does not allow for overdrafts.

If you fail to use the day's deposits, the loss is yours. We cannot borrow from the previous day or ask for a loan from the future.

You must live in the present to reap the benefits of today's deposits. Invest the _time_ that you are given so that you get from it the utmost in health, happiness, and success! The clock is running. Make the most of today; treasure every moment that you have!

"Yesterday is history, tomorrow is a mystery, today is a gift of God, which is why we call it the present!" Bill Keane

"You can make more money but you can't make more time." Anonymous

Have you ever heard the expression, "_time_ is money"? That statement is in fact untrue. _Time_ is much more valuable than money. It may be hard to make more money, but it can be done. But it is totally impossible to make more _time_.

"Time is a resource that is nonrenewable and nontransferable. You cannot store it, slow it up, hold it up, divide it up or give it up. You can't hoard it up or save it for a rainy day— when it's lost it's unrecoverable. When you kill time, remember that it has no resurrection." A.W. Tozer

"Time is the capital that God has given us to invest. People are the stocks in which we are to invest our time, whether they're blue chips or penny stocks or even junk bonds."
Bill Graham

Where you invest your *time* reveals what is most important to you. There are 168 hours in each week. The average person will spend about 56 of those hours sleeping, about 24 of those hours in eating and personal hygiene, and about 50 of those hours working or traveling to work. That means there are only about 35 hours a week of "discretionary" *time* left over. That's about five hours per day.

Question: Where are you investing those hours?

If I were to follow you around and observe you for those five hours, after about 10 days, I could tell you what is most important in your life.

You might not like it, or agree with it, but for some of you, surfing the Internet is most important to you. For others of you, watching television, or reading magazines is what's most important.

How much of that discretionary _time_ are you devoting to your Lord? How much are you devoting to your family? A study of 1,500 households at the University of Michigan found mothers working outside the home spend an average of 11 minutes a day on weekdays, and thirty minutes a day on weekends with the children (not including mealtime). Fathers spend an average of 8 minutes a day on weekdays and 14 minutes a day on weekends in different activities with their children.

Probably many of you know the illustration of the physics teacher who gave his students a wide-mouth mason jar. He then gave them five big rocks, a handful of marbles, a container of sand and a glass of water. He said, "You've got fifteen seconds to put all of these items in the jar."
The physics teacher then stepped back with stopwatch in hand and yelled, "Go!"
The students poured in the sand, threw in the marbles and started stuffing the rocks in. After fifteen seconds he shouted, "Time's up."
There still sitting on the table were three large rocks and the glass of water. The students started complaining, "It can't be done. It's impossible.

*All that stuff will not fit. The jar is too small."
The teacher calmly said, "I can put them all
in the jar." The students responded, "Show
us." So they dumped everything back on the
table – separated everything and started over.
The teacher then took the jar and placed a
couple of the big rocks in the jar. He filled in
any gaps around the big rocks with the
marbles and continued to fill the jar until it
was up to the brim with all the big rocks and
all the marbles. The teacher then took the
sand and slowly poured it into the jar and
watched as it cascaded around the rocks and
the marbles – filling all the holes and spaces.
He then took the glass of water and poured it
into the jar. Everything fit perfectly. He then
said, "It all fits – but it depends on the order
that you put them in the jar – that is a matter
of setting priorities.*

There may not seem like enough time in a
day; to do all of the things that you want to do
on a daily basis. But when something is
important, don't you make time to do it?

So how important is your relationship with
God? Make God a priority. When you set
priorities you can make anything happen.

"Time management is a misleading concept. You can't really manage time. You can't delay it, speed it up, save it or lose it. No matter what you do time keeps moving forward at the same rate. The challenge is not to manage time, but to manage ourselves."
Stephen Covey

Y

You
1: Used to refer to the person or group of people that is being addressed as the subject of a verb or as the object of a verb or preposition
2: Used to refer to any person or to people in general

Proverbs 16:3 (AMP)

*3 Commit your works to the L*ORD *[submit and trust them to Him].*
And your plans will succeed [if you respond to His will and guidance].

When I read this scripture I am reminded of how much power the word "*you*" holds. If *you* are committed, then *you* will be successful. *You* must follow God's word. No one else is responsible for your results, it's all on *you*!

In high school I ran the first leg of the 4x100 meter race.

There are three key rules to a successful relay team. The first rule is to stay in your lane, the second rule is to not drop the baton, and the third rule is the exchange must happen within the permitted zone.

I want to focus on rule number one, stay in your lane. The other teams may be faster than mine, but if they step in my lane they are disqualified. The reverse is true; if I step in their lane I am disqualified. So the only way to win the relay race is to stay in your lane. I wonder how many people out there are trying to win a race in someone else's lane. My mother would often say, "what is for _you_ is for _you_"; this reminds me of a story I once read.

Harby's uncle had gold fever, so he staked his claim and started digging. After a lot of hard work, the uncle found a vein of ore, so he covered up his find and returned home to raise the money for the machinery that he would need to bring the ore to the surface. They raised the money and Darby travelled with his uncle back to the site to make their fortune.
Things started well and before long, they had enough to clear their debts.

They were excited. Everything from here on would be profit and things were looking good. Then the supply of gold stopped. The vein of ore had disappeared.

They kept on digging, but found nothing. After a while, they quit in frustration and sold their machinery to a junk man for a few hundred dollars.

After they went home in disappointment, the astute junk man called in a mining engineer who checked the mine and calculated that there was a vein of gold just three feet from where Darby and his uncle had stopped digging.

The junk man went on to make millions from the mine.

Darby was three feet away from his goal, but he wasn't committed. Remember _you_ are in charge of your destiny and _you_ will be successful as long as _you_ follow His word. Since our time is limited, don't waste it living someone else's life. Work on _you_! Are you following Gods plan or are you making it up as you go along.

Psalm 37:23 (AMP)
The steps of a [good and righteous] man are directed and established by the Lord

John 15:7 (AMP)
If you remain in Me and My words remain in you [that is, if we are vitally united and My message lives in your heart], ask whatever you wish and it will be done for you.

The scripture says your plans will be successful if _you_ follow His will. So if you're not finding success, what is that saying about your plan?

If we can walk in His will, He will pay the bills because it's a part of the plan.

Sometimes part of your plan may lead to _you_ helping someone reach their goals. This is a part of the process; while _you_ are helping them, you will encounter something I call a "jumping off moment". This is the point where your sacrificial help will eventually lead to achieving your own dream. For example, _you_ can help a friend plan a wedding.

A guest may recognize the quality of work and hire _you_ for a larger event. Because _you_ planted a seed, a dream has become a reality.

So in your helping others, _you_ need to also be ready, set, and go when that door opens.

I want to be clear…_YOU_ are the key to your success. Our God has any resource you need to be successful. Now what lane will _you_ travel in?

> _"The best way to find yourself is to lose yourself in the service of others."_
> _Mahatma Gandhi_

> _"Be yourself, but always your better self"_
> _Karl Maeser_

Z

Zoo

1: A place where many kinds of animals are kept so that people can see them

2: A place, situation, or group that is crowded, loud and uncontrolled

Proverbs 6:6-8 (KJV)
6 Go to the ant, thou sluggard; consider her ways, and be wise: 7 Which having no guide, overseer, or ruler, 8 Provideth her meat in the summer, and gathereth her food in the harvest.

Matthew 10:16 (ESV)
16 "Behold, I am sending you out as sheep in the midst of wolves, so be wise as serpents and innocent as doves.

The Bible gives us insight on different characteristics of the animal kingdom that we must imitate.

Whether you believe it or not, we are living in a *zoo*.

"Life is a zoo in a jungle." Peter De Vries

Seriously take a moment and think about this. The world is full of people who have different ambitions and goals. We have to navigate our way through the jungle of life.

The scripture says that we must identify not with just ourselves, but with those around us. In this sense, we must step out of our situations and observe the world around us.

Question: Have you stepped into someone's shoes today?

We are so quick to run our race that we often forget about our fellow racers. Sure, we keep up with the ones closest to us, but what about those in the back of the pack?

"Every morning in Africa, a gazelle wakes up, it knows it must outrun the fastest lion or it will be killed.

Every morning in Africa, a lion wakes up. It knows it must run faster than the slowest gazelle, or it will starve.

It doesn't matter whether you're the lion or a gazelle-when the sun comes up, you'd better be running."

In the <u>zoo</u> of life, we are constantly trying to outrun the next person. We have all heard the saying "Only the Strong Survive"; so the competitor instinct in us is to beat the person behind us.

New Zealand runner Nikki Hamblin was lying on the track, dazed after a heavy fall and with her hopes of an Olympic medal seemingly over. Suddenly, there was a hand on her shoulder and a voice in her ear: "Get up. We have to finish this."
It was American Abbey D'Agostino, offering to help.
"I was like, 'Yup, yup, you're right. This is the Olympic Games. We have to finish this'," Hamblin said.
It was a scene to warm the hearts of fans during a qualifying heat of the women's 5,000 meters. Hamblin and D'Agostino set aside their own hopes of making the final to look out for a fellow competitor.

Sometimes we only get ahead when we reach back and help the person behind. D'Agostino understood that stopping to help Hamblin would cost her a chance at reaching the Olympic Finals. But her compassion for a fellow athlete outweighed her initial goal.

The _zoo_ of life doesn't have to be loud, out of control and ruled by the crab in a barrel mindset. For His word says that we must identify not with just ourselves, but with those around us. In order to survive, we have to work together.

"Zoo: An excellent place to study the habits of human beings." Evan Esar

Conclusion

This book has been my personal love story. I have honed and perfected this message over the years with students from all ages in every environment. When I'm not teaching in church or business environments, I spend my time talking to young people. I believe that our young people have the greatest potential return on investment; they are our future. For the most part they are still moldable and have not developed some of the bad habits us older folk have.

I know this book was a God given message that can impact everybody's life, young or old if you can realign your belief systems. As I mentioned in my first book "*Fully Equipped*", we have all we need to succeed. I believe this book is a seed that will provide a tremendous harvest for years to come. I believe this book will be a resource that you can read and reread to keep you in the optimal mindset to be successful.

I want to leave you with one final quote.

"Success is to be measured not so much by the position that one has reached in life as by the obstacles which he has overcome while trying to succeed." Booker T. Washington

Made in the USA
Columbia, SC
10 February 2018